WHERE IN THE WORLD?

AROUND THE GLOBE IN 13 WORKS OF ART

ASIA

NORTH
AMERICA

Delft, the
Netherlands

Salford,
England

Venice,
Italy

Afghanistan

Paris, France

EUROPE

United States

Harlem,
New York,
USA

Edo,

Mediterranean Sea

Tunis,
Tunisia

ATLANTIC
OCEAN

AFRICA

Tenochtitlán, Mexico

Cotopaxi, Ecuador

SOUTH
AMERICA

BOB RACZKA

INDIAN
OCEAN

PACIFIC
OCEAN

AUSTRALIA

➤ Route
• City
■ Volcano
▲ Mountain

Ⅿ MILLBROOK PRESS • MINNEAPOLIS

To Ethan, who loves geography

Text copyright © 2007 by Bob Raczka

Millbrook Press, Inc.
A division of Lerner Publishing Group
241 First Avenue North
Minneapolis, MN 55401 U.S.A.

Website address: www.lernerbooks.com

Library of Congress Cataloging-in-Publication Data

Raczka, Bob.
    Where in the world? : around the globe in 13 works of art /
  by Bob Raczka.
       p. cm.
    ISBN-13: 978–0–8225–6371–6 (lib. bdg. : alk. paper)
    ISBN-10: 0–8225–6371–1 (lib. bdg. : alk. paper)
    1. Art appreciation—Juvenile literature. I. Title.
  N7440.R332 2007
  709—dc22   2006014895

Manufactured in the United States of America
1 2 3 4 5 6 - JR - 12 11 10 09 08 07

INTRODUCTION

One of my favorite things about art is that it can take you places. I've been to France, the Netherlands, China, Russia, several countries in Africa, even outer space, just by visiting the Art Institute in Chicago where I live.

Not only can art take you to different places, it can take you to different times in history as well. You can experience the Middle Ages in England, the Renaissance in Italy, the Spanish Civil War, or the birth of America, just by looking at a work of art.

With this book, I'd like to take you on a little "world tour." But instead of traveling by plane or by boat or by car, we'll be traveling by art. The only thing you need to pack is your imagination.

We'll be making thirteen stops along the way. And although we won't see every fascinating corner of the world, we will see quite a wide range of landscapes. So find a comfy seat and enjoy the trip.

— Bob Raczka

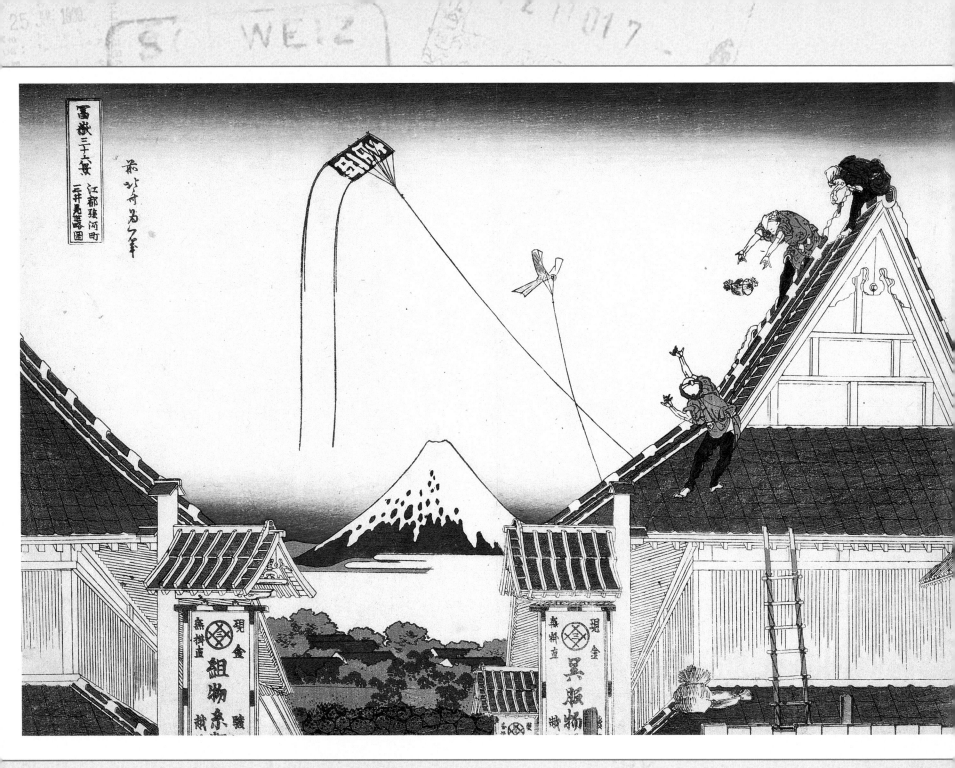

THIRTY-SIX VIEWS OF FUJI: THE MITSUI SHOP AT SURUGACHO IN EDO • 1829–1833 • KATSUSHIKA HOKUSAI
THE NORTON SIMON MUSEUM, PASADENA, CALIFORNIA

EDO, JAPAN

We begin our world tour in Edo, Japan. If you've never heard of Edo, that's not surprising. Edo was the old name for Tokyo, before it became the capital city of Japan.

Katsushika Hokusai was born near Edo in 1760. He became interested in art at a very young age. In his autobiography, he wrote, "From the age of five I have had a mania for sketching the forms of things." By the time he was ten, Hokusai was learning wood-block carving and printmaking. When he died at the age of eighty-nine, he had designed more than thirty thousand wood-block prints.

Hokusai's most famous series of wood-block prints is called *Thirty-Six Views of Mount Fuji*. It actually contains forty-six prints—ten were added at a later date. Mount Fuji is Japan's highest mountain, rising 12,388 feet (3,778 meters) above sea level. It is Japan's most famous landmark and is also a dormant volcano.

In this print from his famous series, Hokusai puts us right in the middle of Edo, on Sugura Street in the 1820s. In front of us is the famous Mitsui drapery shop. Its trademark appears on the hanging banners. On the roof of the shop, workers lay new tiles, and just beyond the workers, two kites hang in the breeze. Mount Fuji looms in the distance, echoing the shape of the shop's roof.

Hokusai made his *Thirty-Six Views of Mount Fuji* between the ages of sixty-four and seventy-two. Many critics consider them to be his best work. Yet he always thought he could do better. When he died, his last words were, "If heaven gives me ten more years, or an extension of even five years, I shall surely become a true artist."

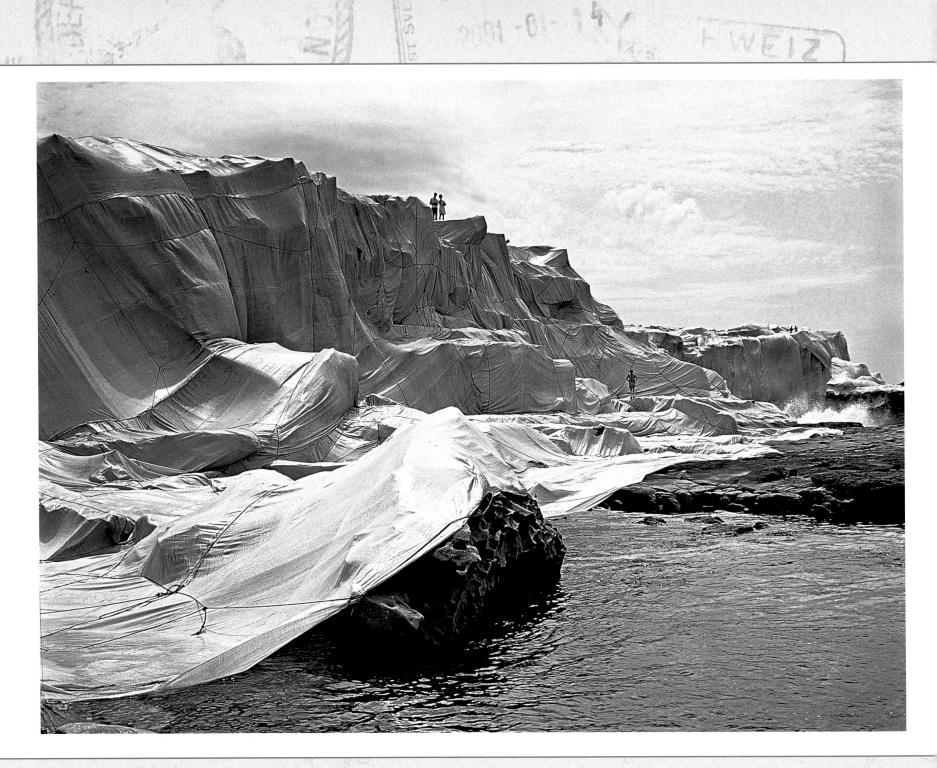

WRAPPED COAST, ONE MILLION SQUARE FEET • 1969 • CHRISTO AND JEANNE-CLAUDE • LITTLE BAY, AUSTRALIA

LITTLE BAY, AUSTRALIA

G'day, and welcome to "the land down under." That's what people call Australia because it is located south of, or down under, the equator. We are actually at a place called Little Bay, which is 9 miles (14.5 kilometers) south of Sydney, Australia's oldest and largest city.

In 1969 the husband-and-wife artist team of Christo and Jeanne-Claude turned Little Bay into a piece of environmental art. To be more specific, they wrapped 1.5 miles (2.4 km) of Little Bay's rocky, cliff-lined coast in one million square feet (93,000 sq. m) of beige-colored fabric.

Not only is this a great example of environmental art, it also shows how art can be created in collaboration. All the drawings and preparation were done by Christo and Jeanne-Claude, but the wrapping itself was completed with the help of 110 laborers and 15 professional rock climbers. The team used 35 miles (56 km) of rope, and to secure the rope, they fired twenty-five thousand fasteners into the rocks using nail guns. It took them four weeks.

So why did they do it? You could say that by wrapping this coastline, Christo and Jeanne-Claude turned it into a "sculpture-scape," forcing you to appreciate the landscape more by making you look at it in a different way. Whatever their intentions were, the wrapping was only temporary. After seven weeks, they returned the coastline to its original state. And all the materials they used were recycled.

It's interesting to note that while Christo and Jeanne-Claude always pay their workers, eleven architecture students who helped out on this project refused to be paid. It was enough for them to contribute to such a unique work of art.

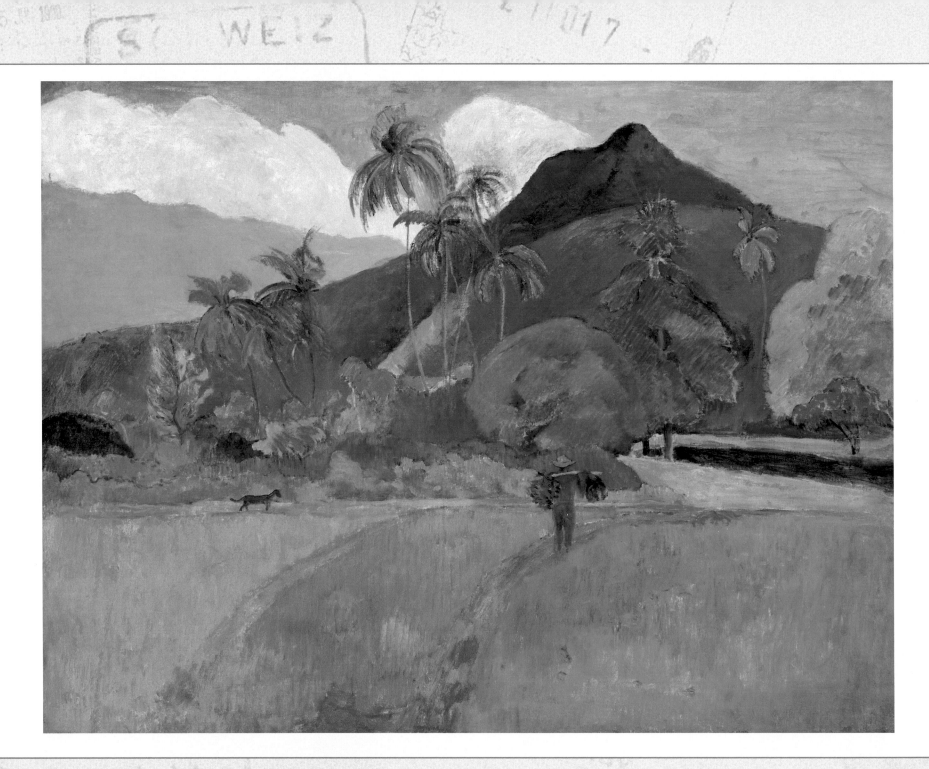

Tahitian Landscape • 1893 • Paul Gauguin • The Minneapolis Institute of Arts, Minneapolis, Minnesota

T A H I T I It would be pretty difficult to get farther away from the rest of the world than Tahiti, which is where we now find ourselves. Tahiti is the biggest island in a chain, or archipelago, called the Society Islands. It's in the middle of the Pacific Ocean, about halfway between Australia and South America.

Tahiti has a tropical climate and is covered in rain forest. The French explorer Louis-Antoine de Bougainville, who wrote a book about his sailing trip around the world, described Tahiti as an earthly paradise. This is exactly what the late-blooming artist Paul Gauguin was looking for when he sailed there in 1891.

Gauguin was born in Paris in 1848, and from the beginning, he was a world traveler. His family moved to Peru in 1849, then back to Paris in 1855. In 1865 he joined the merchant marine, sailing back and forth between France and South America. He even made a voyage around the world.

Gauguin finally settled in Paris. He got a job as a stockbroker and had a family. He also dabbled in painting, an interest that became more serious when he met Camille Pissarro and the other Impressionists. His stockbroker job allowed him to buy many of their works. But, eventually, he left behind the business world, his Impressionist friends, and even his family to find his own way as a painter.

This landscape was painted a couple of years after Gauguin arrived in Tahiti. By this time, he had achieved his own style, which he called Symbolism. It was a combination of bold compositions, flat planes, and brilliantly bright colors, no doubt influenced by Tahiti's tropical sunlight.

Gauguin died on a nearby island, in a cabin he called the House of Joy. This seems appropriate, since his colorful paintings bring joy to anyone who sees them. ✹

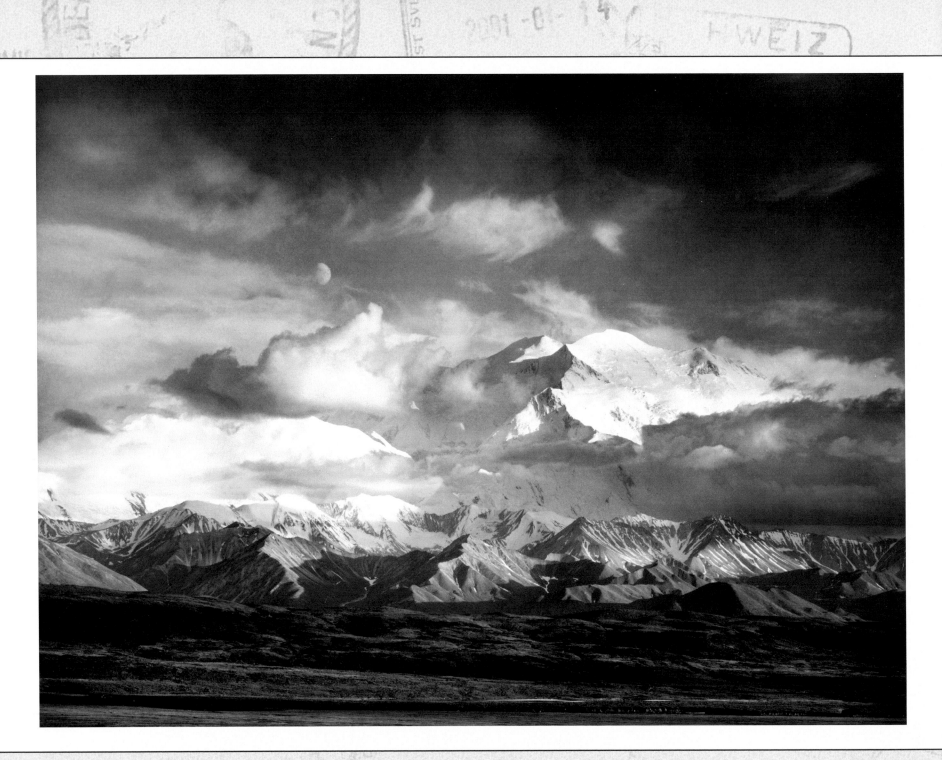

Moon and Mount McKinley, Denali National Park • 1947 • Photograph by Ansel Adams
The Ansel Adams Publishing Rights Trust, Mill Valley, California

MOUNT McKINLEY, ALASKA

Next, we head to Alaska, the largest of the fifty United States. It's also the home of the tallest mountain in North America, Mount McKinley, which reaches 20,320 feet (6,198 m) into the sky. The native Athabaskan Indians called it Denali, which means "The High One." Mount McKinley, or Denali, is part of Denali National Park, which protects about thirty different animal species and over eighty kinds of birds.

The unofficial photographer of America's national parks was Ansel Adams, who was born in San Francisco in 1902. When he was fourteen, he started taking photos in nearby Yosemite National Park with a camera he received as a gift. Adams also developed a love for exploring, hiking, and climbing at Yosemite. When he was seventeen, he joined the environmental group, the Sierra Club. And by 1948, Adams was working on a project to photograph all of the national parks in the United States.

Adams worked mostly in black and white. He believed in pure photography and was against photos that looked like Impressionist paintings or etchings. He preferred images in sharp focus, with a wide range of grays, blacks, and whites.

This photo of Mount McKinley is a great example of how Adams played with light. Our eyes move from the nearly black plains at the bottom, to the gray foothills, to the white clouds and mountain peaks, then up to the gray sky and, finally, back to near blackness at the top. And hovering like a ghost is the moon.

Although he was an artist first, Adams was proud that his photos helped educate people about the environment. He once said, "It is horrifying that we have to fight our own government to save the environment." In 1985, the year after he died, a peak in California's Sierra Nevada range was named Mount Ansel Adams in his honor.

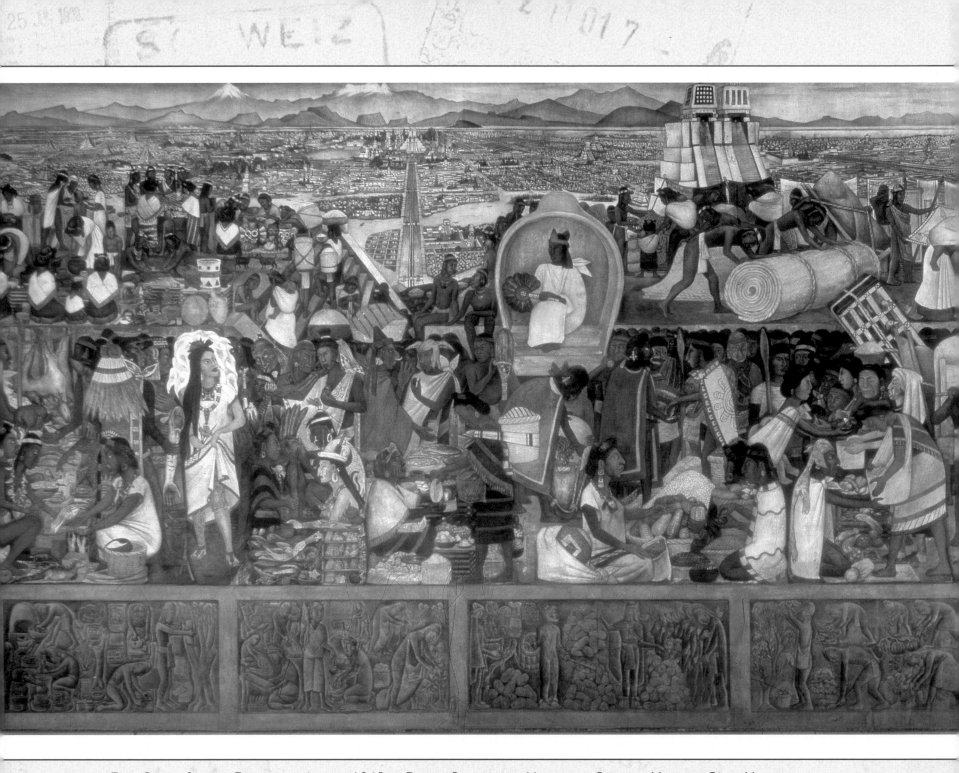

THE GREAT CITY OF TENOCHTITLÁN • 1945 • DIEGO RIVERA • NATIONAL PALACE, MEXICO CITY, MEXICO

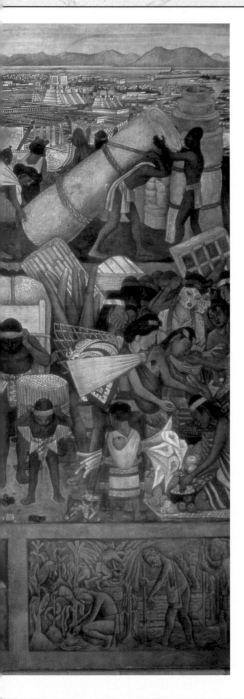

TENOCHTITLÁN, MEXICO

We've just traveled more than five hundred years back in time to Tenochtitlán, the capital of the Aztec Empire. Tenochtitlán was built in the early fourteenth century on a small island in the middle of Lake Texcoco. Over time, the Aztecs enlarged the city by planting floating gardens, or *chinampas*, then connecting them with canals and causeways, called *calzadas*. Tenochtitlán was one of the largest cities in the world when the Spanish conquistador Hernando Cortés arrived in 1519. Cortés and his army conquered the city in 1521. Mexico City, today's capital of Mexico, was built on its ruins.

Diego Rivera was six years old when his family moved to Mexico City in 1892. As a boy, he showed great artistic talent, and when he was twenty, he won a scholarship to study art in Spain. Rivera stayed in Europe for fourteen years, traveling to France, Belgium, the Netherlands, Great Britain, and Italy. He studied many artistic styles and techniques, including the wall and ceiling murals, or frescoes, of the Italian Renaissance.

When he returned to Mexico in 1921, Rivera became intrigued by the art of native Mexican civilizations like the Aztec. He tried his first mural, and before long, he mastered the fresco technique of painting on wet plaster. Eventually, he developed his own bold and colorful style. Rivera believed art should serve the common people, so he focused on painting important moments from Mexican history in large public spaces.

In this mural, Rivera shows us the bustling city of Tenochtitlán as it might have looked during the 1400s. In the foreground, we see the colorfully dressed Aztec people working, trading, and conversing. In the background is the city itself, with its impressive network of floating gardens, causeways, and temple pyramids.

Rivera died in 1957, having become part of the Mexican history he loved to paint.

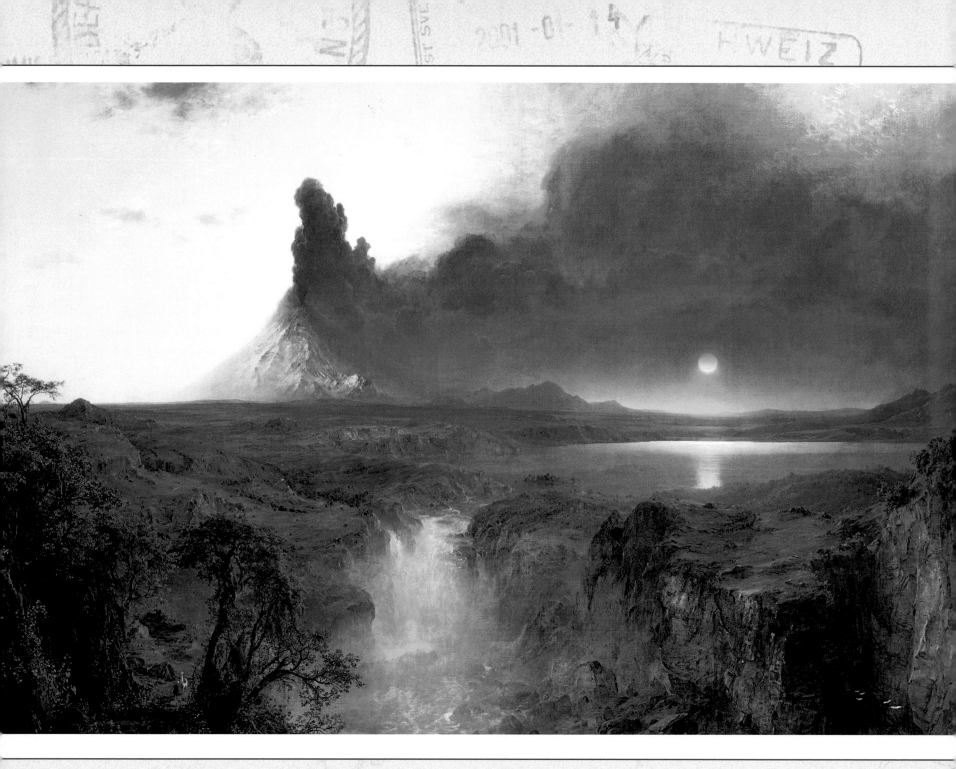

Cotopaxi • 1862 • Frederick Edwin Church • The Detroit Institute of Arts, Detroit, Michigan

COTOPAXI, ECUADOR

We now find ourselves in Ecuador, one of the smallest countries in South America. *Ecuador* is the Spanish word for "equator," and in fact, the equator passes right through it. The Inca Indians once ruled over much of Ecuador, until 1534, when they were conquered by Francisco Pizarro and his Spanish army.

The central part of Ecuador is dominated by the Andes mountain range. Cotopaxi, the volcano we see here, is part of that range. It lies about 40 miles (64 km) south of Quito, Ecuador's capital. Cotopaxi is the second-highest volcano in the country, and in Quechua, the language of the Incas, it means "smooth neck of the moon."

The first North American artist to visit South America was Frederick Edwin Church. Born in Connecticut, Church was the son of a wealthy man, which made it possible for him to study drawing and painting at a young age. When he was eighteen, Church became the first pupil of Thomas Cole, the leading U.S. landscape painter at that time. According to Cole, Church had "the finest eye for drawing in the world."

Inspired by the writings of Alexander von Humboldt, a German naturalist and explorer, Church traveled all over the world. This was a time of expansion and optimism in the United States. Church's detailed views of everything from icebergs to waterfalls to volcanoes soon made him the nation's most famous painter.

It was after his second trip to Ecuador that Church painted this view of Cotopaxi erupting. Because it was painted in 1862, some people think that this landscape, with its overwhelming red color and dark clouds of smoke in the background, symbolizes the bloody Civil War that had just erupted in the United States.

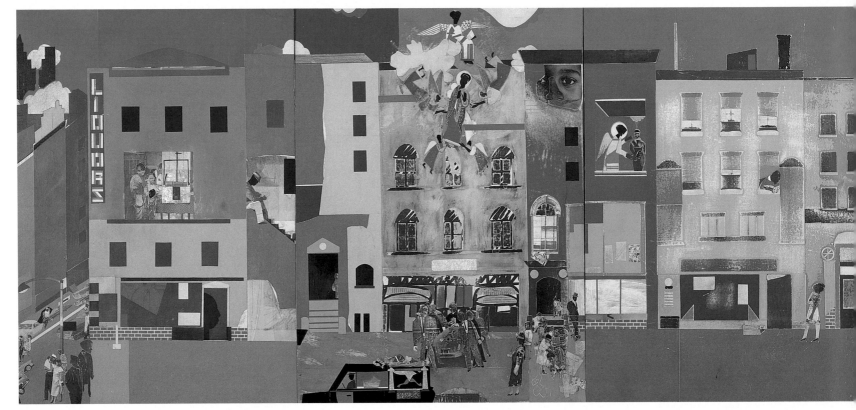

THE BLOCK • 1971 • ROMARE BEARDEN • THE METROPOLITAN MUSEUM OF ART, NEW YORK, NEW YORK

HARLEM, NEW YORK

The neighborhood of Harlem in New York City is one of the unique stops on our tour. It was originally settled by the Dutch in the mid-1600s. They called the area New Haarlem, after the city of Haarlem in the Netherlands. Eventually, the *New* and the second *a* were dropped, and by the early 1900s, Harlem had become primarily an African American neighborhood.

Romare Bearden's family moved to Harlem when he was three. He was lucky enough to grow up during the Harlem Renaissance, a time of incredible artistic growth for African American culture. Bearden's parents were very involved in Harlem's cultural life, and as a boy, he met many famous people, including jazz musician Duke Ellington, poet Langston Hughes, writer W. E. B. Du Bois, and painter Aaron Douglas.

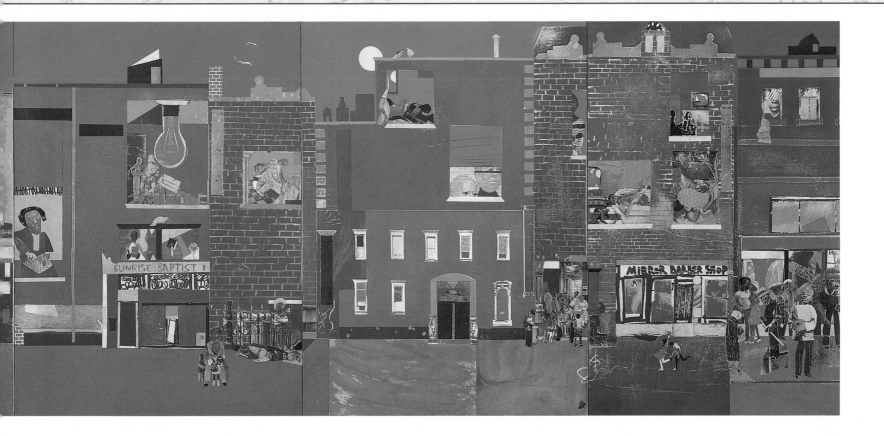

As a result of this upbringing, Bearden had many interests. He earned a degree in mathematics. He studied painting, art history, and philosophy. He was a writer, a cartoonist, and a social worker. He loved jazz music. And he experimented with many different styles of art. He finally settled on collage as his favorite, which seems appropriate for a man whose own life was like a collage.

This work is a tribute to the neighborhood that inspired him. To create it, Bearden used fabric, colored paper, foil, and photographs, as well as pencils, markers, paint, and ink. It shows people attending a funeral, caring for children, and just hanging out. We can see a church, a barbershop, and a corner grocery store. As Bearden once said, "I think of Harlem as a young boy as a place of great energy." And it shows. 🕸

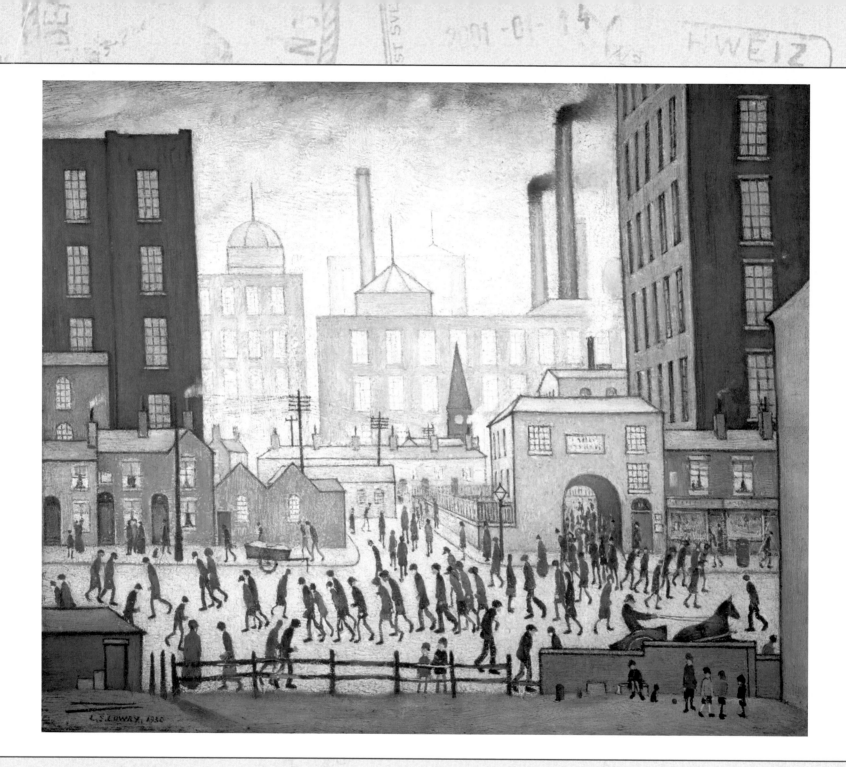

COMING FROM THE MILL • 1930 • L. S. LOWRY • THE LOWRY, SALFORD QUAYS, ENGLAND

SALFORD, ENGLAND

In the northern part of England, on the River Irwell, lies the town of Salford. During the Industrial Revolution of the 1700s and early 1800s, many factories and mills were built here, and Salford became one of England's first industrial cities. But while these factories made it easier to manufacture products, they also created many problems, such as pollution, overcrowding, and an entire class of factory workers who lived in poverty because they were overworked and underpaid.

L. S. (Laurence Stephen) Lowry was born near Salford in 1887. As a boy, Lowry didn't make many friends, wasn't a good student, and didn't know what he wanted to do with his life. But his aunt noticed that he was good at drawing ships, so when he was fifteen, Lowry's parents signed him up for private art lessons. He made art for the rest of his life.

Lowry never paid much attention to the nearby factories until 1909, when his family moved to one of Salford's industrial areas. At this time, he took a job as a rent collector, knocking on the doors of the poor factory workers and seeing firsthand what their lives were like. As he said later, "I saw the industrial scene and was affected by it. I tried to paint it all the time."

So the life of the factory worker became his subject. In this painting, we see mill workers heading for home. And even though the sky is dirty, the colors are muted, and the workers are painted with very few brushtrokes, it is not depressing. These people are very much alive, and we can tell that Lowry is rooting for them.

Before he died, Lowry made nearly one thousand paintings and more than eight thousand drawings. You'll find many of his works at the The Lowry, Salford Quays, a multipurpose arts complex named in his memory.

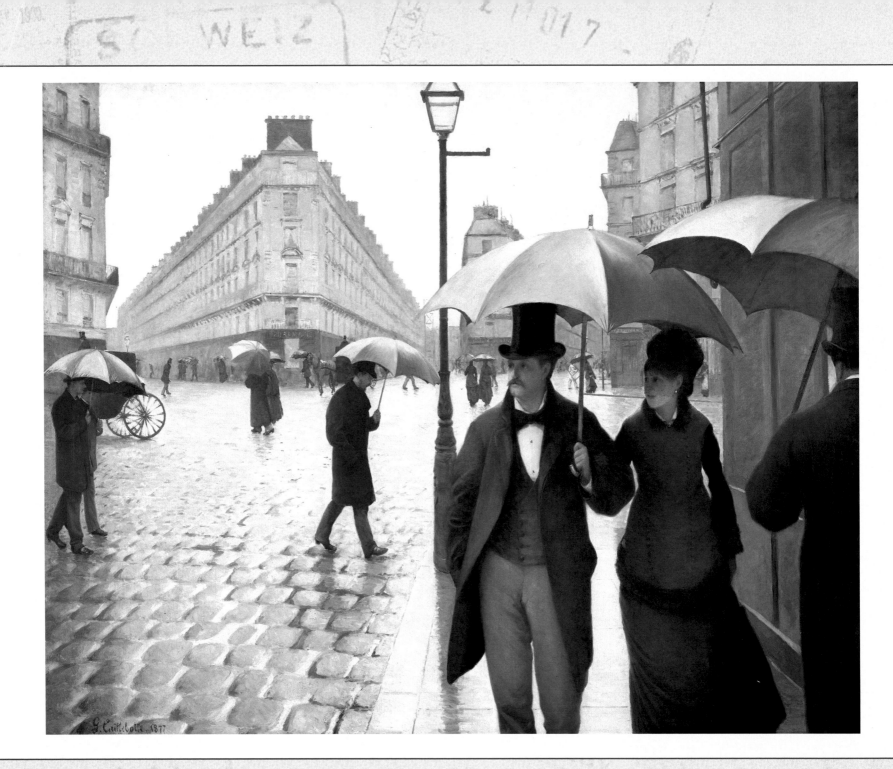

PARIS STREET; RAINY DAY · 1877 · GUSTAVE CAILLEBOTTE · THE ART INSTITUTE OF CHICAGO, CHICAGO, ILLINOIS

PARIS, FRANCE

Welcome to Paris, France, in the year 1877. I hope you brought your umbrella, because when you stand in front of this huge painting, which measures almost 7 feet (213 centimeters) high by 9 feet (275 cm) wide, you feel like one of the Parisians on the street getting wet.

This work is by Gustave Caillebotte, who was born in Paris in 1848. He is closely associated with the Impressionists, and he even exhibited with them, but his style was much more realistic than theirs. Caillebotte came from a wealthy family, and unlike most artists, he didn't need to sell his work to make a living.

When his father died in 1874, Caillebotte inherited a large sum of money. During that same year, he became friends with the Impressionists Edgar Degas, Claude Monet, and Pierre-Auguste Renoir. Caillebotte used his inheritance to support his artist friends. He organized and financed their exhibitions, and he often bought their paintings for his own collection. In fact, until recently he was better known as a patron of the arts than as an artist himself.

During Caillebotte's lifetime, Paris was transformed into a modern capital city, with wide avenues replacing the narrow streets of the past. This painting is a wonderful example of what the updated city looked like. Caillebotte shows us fashionably dressed men and women strolling along one of the new boulevards, with several of the latest, modern-looking buildings in the background.

Caillebotte died when he was just forty-five years old, but his generosity did not end with his death. In his will, he left his entire collection of Impressionist paintings to the French government.

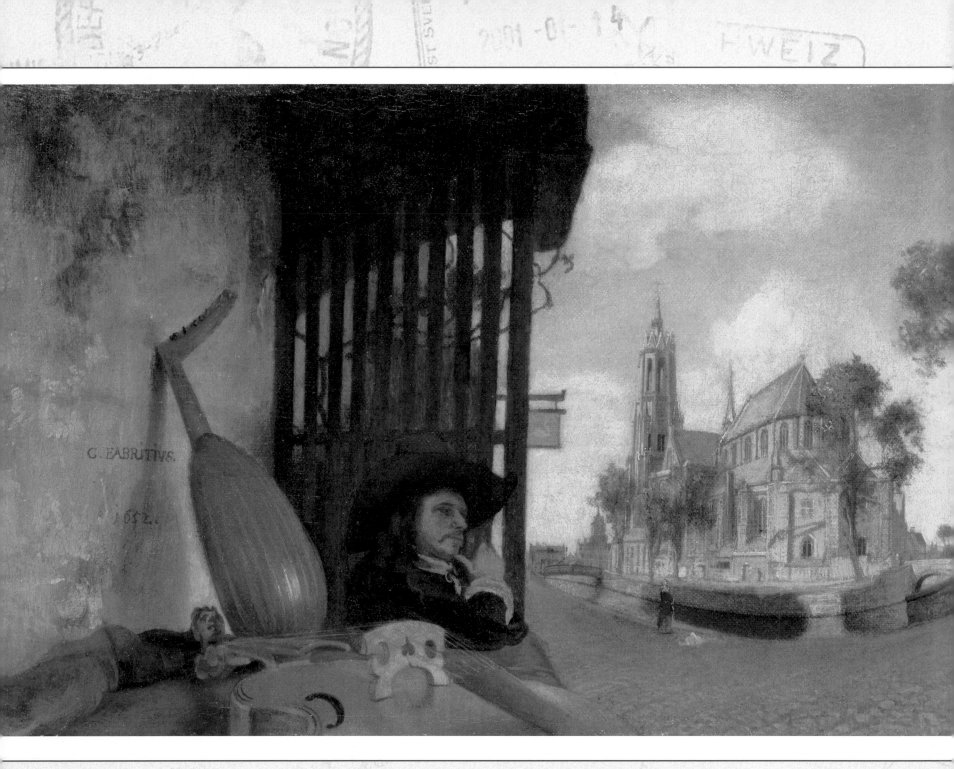

A View of Delft with a Musical Instrument Seller's Stall • 1652 • Carel Fabritius
The National Gallery, London, England

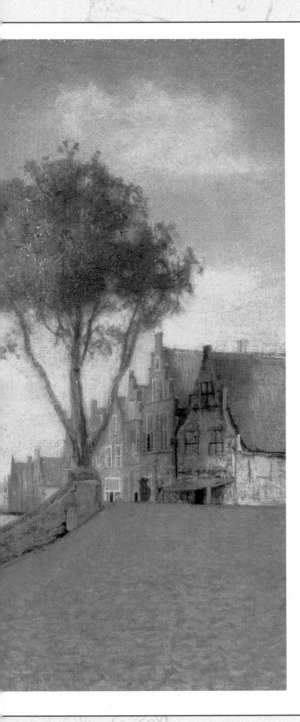

DELFT, THE NETHERLANDS

Our next stop is the Dutch city of Delft, in the Netherlands. This painting of Delft was made in 1652, during the Dutch Golden Age. At this time, the Netherlands was a prosperous seafaring and trading nation. Many Dutch people had money to spend on art, and many great artists lived during this time, including Rembrandt van Rijn and Jan Vermeer.

In fact, the artist who made this painting, Carel Fabritius, was a student of Rembrandt. Historians also believe he taught Vermeer. Fabritius might have become as famous as they did, but he died in 1654, when the gunpowder arsenal in Delft exploded. He was just thirty-two years old. An entire quarter of the city was destroyed, and much of Fabritius's work was lost.

This is one of his twelve paintings that survived. In the foreground, we see a man selling musical instruments. He has a lute and a viola da gamba, which is like a cello, on display. In the center is the Nieuwe Kerk, or "New Church," and winding around the church is a cobblestone street, as well as one of Delft's many canals.

Because this painting has such a long, narrow shape and such a strange, curving perspective, art historians think it might have been part of a special box called a peep show. For a peep show, the artist would paint his scene on the inside walls of a box, and the viewer would look into the box through a special peephole on the outside. This made the painting look more three-dimensional and, thus, more realistic—sort of like a seventeenth-century Dutch diorama!

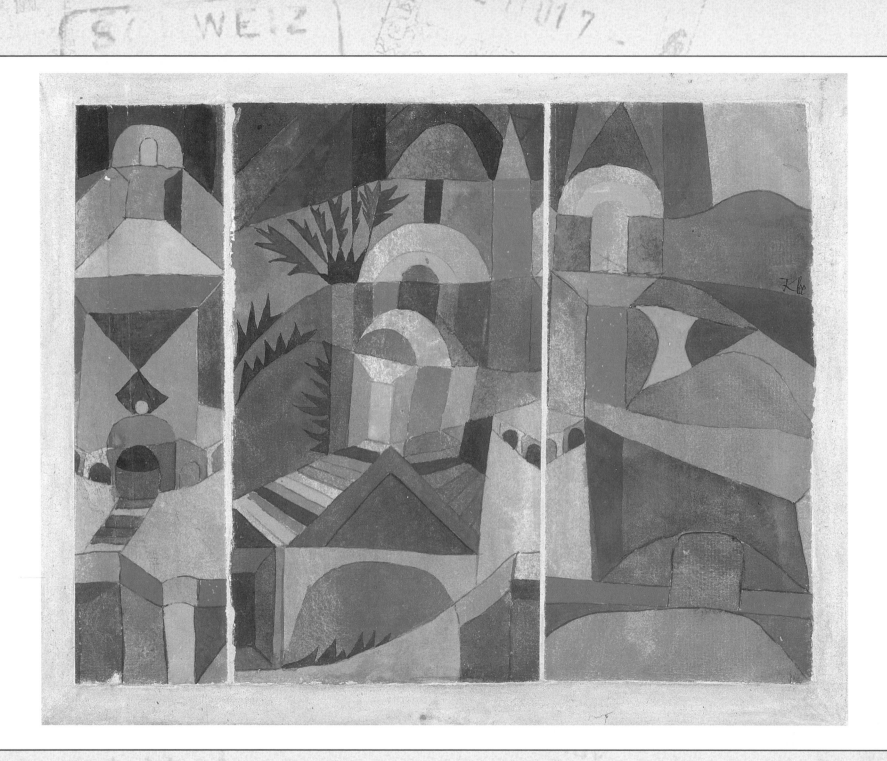

TEMPLE GARDENS • 1920 • PAUL KLEE • THE METROPOLITAN MUSEUM OF ART, NEW YORK, NEW YORK

TUNIS, TUNISIA

No world tour would be complete without a visit to Africa. Tunisia is a small country at the north end of this massive continent, sandwiched between Algeria and Libya, on the coast of the Mediterranean Sea. The Sahara covers most of Tunisia's southern half, but the north, where we are now, is quite fertile.

Tunisia is an Arabic-speaking country. It was originally settled by tribes of people called Berbers, and in their native language, the word *tunis* (which is also the name of the capital of Tunisia) means, "to spend the night." In 1914 the artist Paul Klee spent two weeks in Tunisia, and the visit changed his work forever.

Paul Klee was born in Switzerland in 1879. As a boy, he loved both music and art, and even though he was a master violinist, he chose to concentrate on art. Klee studied in both Germany and Italy, and among his many influences were the German painter August Macke and the Russian painter Wassily Kandinsky.

But the single biggest influence on Klee's art was his trip to Tunisia. Upon arriving at the port city of Tunis, he was so impressed with the strong African light, he wrote in his diary, "The sun has a dark power." Klee claimed to discover color here, and toward the end of his trip, after touring and painting in several Tunisian cities, he wrote, "Color and I are one. I am a painter."

In this colorful painting, which looks like a stained-glass window, Klee shares his impression of the medina, or old section, of a typical Tunisian city. Using simple, nearly abstract shapes, he shows us a maze of stairways, towers, walled gardens, and palm trees. Amazingly, Klee cut the painting into three pieces and moved the middle section to the left, to further capture the mazelike feel of the medina. For the rest of Klee's life, his work would show references to this trip.

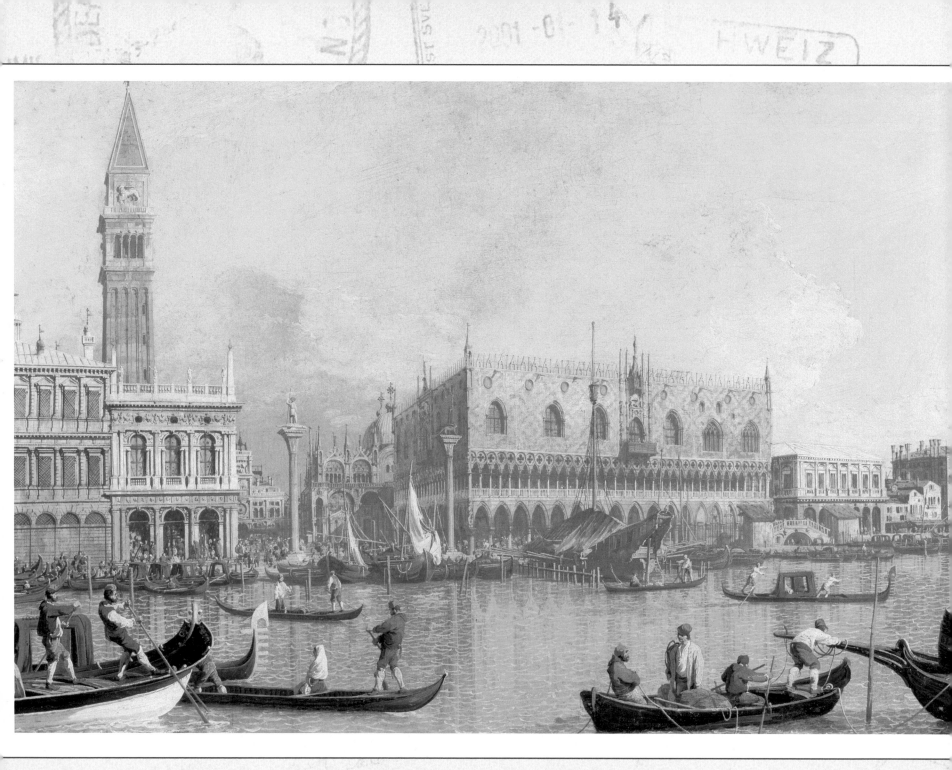

VIEW OF THE DUCAL PALACE, VENICE · 1755 · CANALETTO · GALLERIA DEGLI UFFIZI, FLORENCE, ITALY

VENICE, ITALY

You have just arrived in Venice in the year 1755. Located at the north end of Italy in a lagoon of the Adriatic Sea, Venice is actually a group of islands connected by more than four hundred bridges. Instead of streets, it has more than 150 canals. Thanks to its unusual geography, Venice has always been popular with tourists, who come to ride in skinny, flat-bottomed boats called gondolas and to admire Venice's ornate architecture.

Believe it or not, the man who became famous for painting the city of canals was named Giovanni Antonio Canal. Better known as Canaletto, he was born in Venice in 1697 and died there in 1768. Like his father, Canaletto started out as a painter of scenery for the theater. Eventually he made a career out of painting picturesque views of the city, called *vedute*, for wealthy English tourists.

In this painting of the Grand Canal, which is like the main street of Venice, Canaletto focuses on the Ducal Palace. This was the home of the city's ruler, called the doge. As you can see, the palace has a reddish tint, which comes from the rose-colored marble used to decorate it. And if you're wondering why the gondoliers are all standing in their boats, it's because they use a single, narrow oar called a sweep. This oar is very long, so that when the canals are shallow, the gondolier can use it like a pole to push his boat through the water.

As he grew older, Canaletto was criticized for painting the same scenes over and over again. However, five years before he died, he was elected into the Venetian Academy. Strangely enough, if you traveled to Venice today, you would not see much of Canaletto's work. Due to his popularity with English travelers, most of his paintings ended up in England.

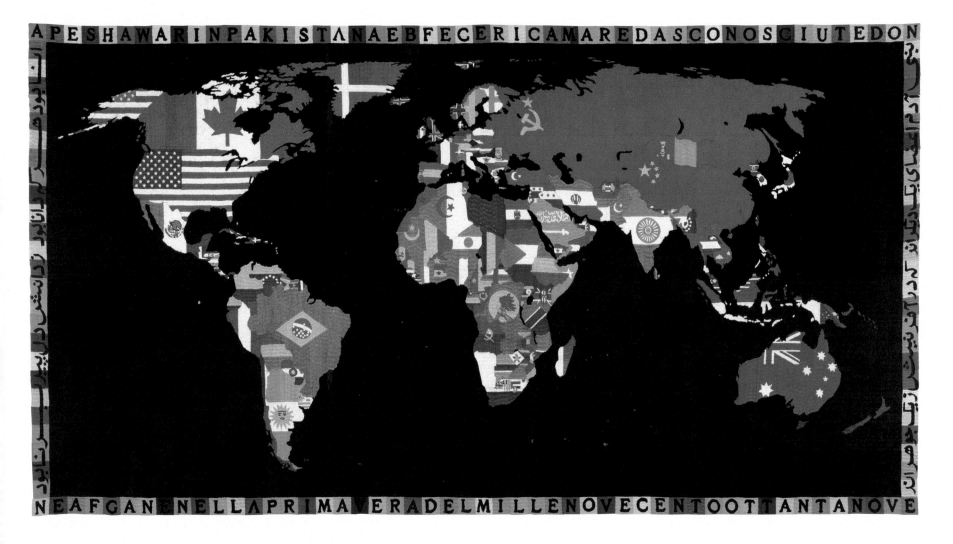

Mappa del Mondo (Map of the World) • 1989 • Alighiero e Boetti • Galleria Franz Paludetto, Turin, Italy

T H E   W O R L D Now that we've been all over the globe, our tour ends with a map of the world. But unlike most maps, which are made of paper, this one is made of embroidered cloth. And as you can see, instead of being filled in with rivers and mountains or cities and highways, the outline of each country is filled in with its flag.

This map was the idea of Alighiero e Boetti, an artist who was born in Italy in 1940 and died there in 1994. An original thinker, Boetti often played with the idea that everything has two sides. For example, he saw the world divided into order and disorder, east and west, artificial and natural, and so on. He even thought of himself as having two sides. In fact, when he was twenty-eight years old, he added the word *and* between his first and last names (e means "and" in Italian).

Boetti also loved to travel. In 1971 he made a trip to Afghanistan, where he was impressed with the rug-weaving skills of the Afghani women. The tradition of rug weaving is thousands of years old there, and it gave Boetti an idea. He would design maps of the world using flags to represent countries, and he would hire groups of Afghani women to create them using traditional rug-weaving techniques.

The result is a work of art that has two sides, modern (the map of today's world) and ancient (the weaving process). And by representing each country with its flag, Boetti reminds us that countries and borders are not natural but man-made things. After all, the earth doesn't look like this from outer space.

But perhaps most important, Boetti's map shows us that people from completely different countries and cultures, such as Italy and Afghanistan, can ignore artificial borders and work together to create beautiful works of art. 🎡

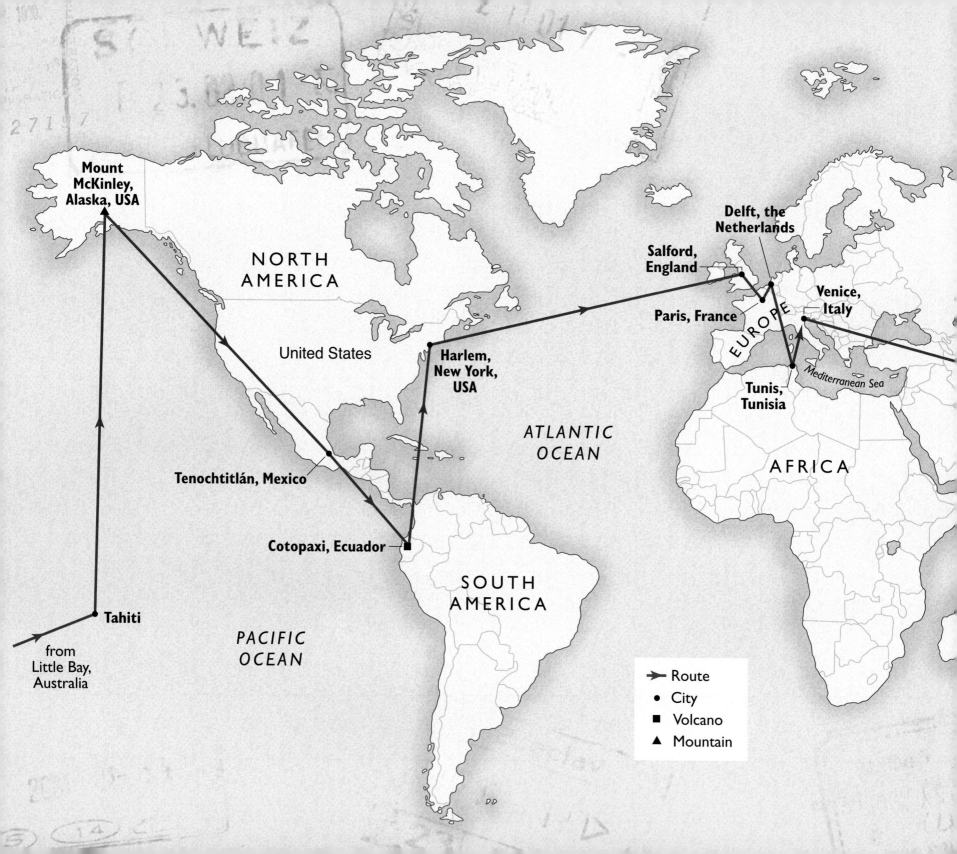

Mount McKinley, Alaska, USA

NORTH AMERICA

United States

Harlem, New York, USA

Delft, the Netherlands

Salford, England

Paris, France

Venice, Italy

EUROPE

Tunis, Tunisia

Mediterranean Sea

AFRICA

ATLANTIC OCEAN

Tenochtitlán, Mexico

Cotopaxi, Ecuador

SOUTH AMERICA

Tahiti

from Little Bay, Australia

PACIFIC OCEAN

✈	Route
●	City
■	Volcano
▲	Mountain

ASIA

Afghanistan

Edo, Japan

PACIFIC
OCEAN

INDIAN
OCEAN

to Tahiti

AUSTRALIA

Little Bay,
Australia

RACZKA'S ROUTE

Start in Edo, Japan

Edo to Little Bay, Australia	4,854 miles (7,815 km)
Little Bay to Tahiti	3,801 miles (6,120 km)
Tahiti to Mount McKinley, Alaska	5,605 miles (9,024 km)
Alaska to Tenochtitlán, Mexico	3,831 miles (6,167 km)
Tenochtitlán to Cotopaxi, Ecuador	1,944 miles (3,130 km)
Cotopaxi to Harlem, New York	2,822 miles (4,543 km)
Harlem to Salford, England	3,346 miles (5,387 km)
Salford to Paris, France	376 miles (605 km)
Paris to Delft, the Netherlands	231 miles (372 km)
Delft to Tunis, Tunisia	1,077 miles (1,734 km)
Tunis to Venice, Italy	601 miles (968 km)
Venice to Afghanistan	3,045 miles (4,902 km)
TOTAL MILES TRAVELED	31,533 miles (50,767 km)

30 30

31

Source notes for quoted material: p. 5, "Hokusai 1760–1849," *artelino—Art Auctions*, n.d., http://www.artelino.com/articles/hokusai.asp (October 14, 2005); p. 5, "Hokusai Katsushika (1760–1849)," *Monash University—Jim Breen's Ukiyo-E Gallery—Hokusai*, n.d., http://www.csse.monash.edu.au/~jwb/ukiyoe/raf_hokusai_intro.html (October 12, 2005); p. 11, "Ansel Adams Quotes," *BrainyQuote*, n.d., http://www.brainyquote.com/quotes/authors/a/ansel_adams.html (December 1, 2005); p. 15, "Artist Summary—Frederic Edwin (1826) Church—1826–1900," *Artfact*, n.d., http://www.artfact.com/features/viewArtist.cfm?aID=1645 (August 4, 2005); p. 17, "Romare Bearden—Guided Tour," *The Metropolitan Museum of Art*, n.d., http://www.metmuseum.org/explore/the_block/guide.html (October 14, 2005); p. 19, "Lowry's Life—Art School 1905," *The Lowry*, n.d., www.thelowry.com/lslowry/lslowryslife.html (September, 2005); p. 25, "Travels in Tunisia," *Saudi Aramco World,* May/June 1991, http://www.saudiaramcoworld.com/issue/199103/travels.in.tunisia.htm (August 4, 2005); p. 25, "Klee, Paul," *WebMuseum, Paris,* n.d., http://www.ibiblio.org/wm/paint/auth/klee/ (November 1, 2005).